Preserving Loui Legacy
Everyone Can Help

Nancy W. Hawkins

Alpha Editions

This edition published in 2024

ISBN 9789362092281

Design and Setting By

Alpha Editions

www.alphaedis.com

Email - info@alphaedis.com

As per information held with us this book is in Public Domain. This book is a reproduction of an important historical work. Alpha Editions uses the best technology to reproduce historical work in the same manner it was first published to preserve its original nature. Any marks or number seen are left intentionally to preserve.

Contents

Editor's Note ....- 1 -

ACKNOWLEDGEMENTS ....- 5 -

ARCHAEOLOGY IN LOUISIANA ....- 6 -

HOW AN ARCHAEOLOGIST STUDIES THE PAST ....- 9 -

MAJOR IMPACTS ON SITE PRESERVATION ....- 13 -

GOVERNMENT HELPS ....- 18 -

BUSINESS AND INDUSTRY HELP ....- 20 -

PRIVATE LANDOWNERS HELP ....- 23 -

YOU CAN HELP ....- 25 -

Editor's Note

Louisiana's cultural heritage dates back to approximately 10,000 B.C. when Paleo-Indian hunters entered the region in search of Pleistocene big game. Since that time, many other groups have settled in the area. Each of these groups has left evidence of its presence in the archaeological record. The Anthropological Study series published by the Department of Culture, Recreation & Tourism provides a readable account of various activities of these cultural groups.

Nancy Hawkins, outreach coordinator for the Division of Archaeology, is the author of *Preserving Louisiana's Legacy*, the fifth volume in the Anthropological Study series. This volume departs somewhat from the previous ones in the series in that it does not describe a particular group of people or archaeological sites. Rather it addresses archaeological preservation as a whole. In this volume Ms. Hawkins explains in general terms how an archaeologist studies the past, what factors affect the preservation of archaeological remains, and how government, industry, business, landowners, and other groups and individuals can contribute to the preservation of Louisiana's archaeological heritage.

We are pleased to be able to make *Preserving Louisiana's Legacy* available and trust that the reader will enjoy this volume.

Kathleen Byrd *State Archaeologist*

STATE OF LOUISIANA
DEPARTMENT OF CULTURE, RECREATION AND TOURISM
OFFICE OF PROGRAM DEVELOPMENT

DAVID C. TREEN
Governor

ROBERT B. DeBLIEUX
Assistant Secretary

MRS. LAWRENCE H. FOX
Secretary

April 20, 1982

CITIZENS OF LOUISIANA

As Louisiana's State Historic Preservation Officer, I am pleased to introduce Preserving Louisiana's Legacy, the fifth volume in the Anthropological Study series of the Department of Culture, Recreation & Tourism and the Louisiana Archaeological Survey & Antiquities Commission.

Through my work first in private business and more recently in local and state government, I have become increasingly impressed with the diversity and uniqueness of Louisiana's archaeological remains. There is no question that many of these archaeological sites should be preserved for the future. They are Louisiana's past.

Louisiana has some of the most important sites in the United States. In fact, one prehistoric archaeological site, Poverty Point in West Carroll Parish, has been suggested for nomination to the World Heritage List. This program, in which 45 nations participate, recognizes areas of outstanding universal value to mankind.

I am proud to live in a state with such a rich archaeological heritage, and I hope that it can be protected for future generations. However, no one individual or group working alone can preserve Louisiana's legacy. Only through the concerted efforts of government, industry, business, and individuals can this be accomplished. This volume suggests what you can do to preserve Louisiana's archaeological sites. I hope you enjoy this booklet.

Sincerely,

ROBERT B. DEBLIEUX
STATE HISTORIC PRESERVATION OFFICER

P. O. Box 44247   Baton Rouge, La. 70804   504-342-6682

STATE OF LOUISIANA
DEPARTMENT OF CULTURE, RECREATION AND TOURISM
OFFICE OF PROGRAM DEVELOPMENT

DAVID C. TREEN
Governor Assistant
ROBERT B. DeBLIEUX
Secretary
MRS. LAWRENCE H. FOX
Secretary

April 20, 1982

CITIZENS OF LOUISIANA

As Louisiana's State Historic Preservation Officer, I am pleased to introduce

Preserving Louisiana's Legacy, the fifth volume in the Anthropological

Study series of the Department of Culture, Recreation & Tourism and the

Louisiana Archaeological Survey & Antiquities Commission.

Through my work first in private business and more recently in local and

state government, I have become increasingly impressed with the diversity

and uniqueness of Louisiana's archaeological remains. There is no question

that many of these archaeological sites should be preserved for the future.

They are Louisiana's past.

Louisiana has some of the most important sites in the United States. In

fact, one prehistoric archaeological site, Poverty Point in West Carroll

Parish, has been suggested for nomination to the World Heritage List.

This program, in which 45 nations participate, recognizes areas of outstanding

universal value to mankind.

I am proud to live in a state with such a rich archaeological heritage,

and I hope that it can be protected for future generations. However, no

one individual or group working alone can preserve Louisiana's legacy.

Only through the concerted efforts of government, industry, business, and individuals can this be accomplished. This volume suggests what you can

do to preserve Louisiana's archaeological sites. I hope you enjoy this

booklet.

Sincerely,

Rob DeBlieux

ROBERT B. DEBLIEUX

STATE HISTORIC PRESERVATION OFFICER

P. O. Box 44247 Baton Rouge, La. 70804 504-342-6682

ACKNOWLEDGEMENTS

Illustrations for this booklet have been generously contributed by several people. Robert Neuman, Louisiana State University, provided photographs of Monk's Mound (cover), a projectile point (p. 1), a vessel from the Clarence H. Webb Collection (p. 2), a shell midden (p. 2), and of excavation pits (p. 15). Debbie Woodiel, State Parks, gave permission to use an illustration from her thesis (p. 5). The American Museum of Natural History permitted reproduction of the Poverty Point site map (p. 1), and New Orleans East provided the illustration on page 13. All other photographs are from the files at the Division of Archaeology, and have been taken by staff archaeologists through the years.

ARCHAEOLOGY IN LOUISIANA

People lived in Louisiana thousands of years before the first Europeans sailed to the New World. Because of archaeology, the history of even these early Indians is now being described and understood. All people leave traces of their activities wherever they cook, build houses, hold religious ceremonies, make tools, or dump their trash. If these traces are undisturbed, archaeologists can use them to determine who left them, when they were left, and what activities were associated with them. These are a few of the things archaeologists have learned about Louisiana:

Although many people refer to all stone points as arrowheads, Indians actually made projectile points for over 10,000 years before they ever used one on an arrow. The point pictured here would have been used on a spear and could have killed a prehistoric elephant, called a mastodon.

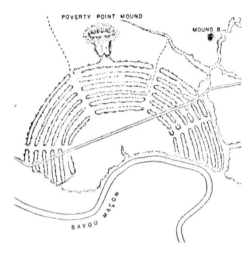

In northeastern Louisiana by 1000 B.C., Indians had built rows of earthen ridges three-quarters of a mile across. As far as we know, they are the earliest earthworks of their size in North America. Some archaeologists think they were constructed as an astronomical observatory because two gaps in the ridges line up with the winter and summer solstice sunsets.

Contrary to present day practice, prehistoric Louisianians preferred marsh clams over crawfish and crabs. They ate so many clams that large piles of shells can still be found in the marshes. Over time, the shells have become compressed, and now some piles are almost rock hard.

Indians in Louisiana made beautiful and elaborate pottery without ever using a potter's wheel. This delicate water bottle was made in northwestern Louisiana about A.D. 1400.

European missionaries and explorers who traveled in Louisiana in the 1600s and 1700s depended on experienced Indian traders to supply them with food, animal skins, salt, and horses. In exchange, Europeans gave the Indians beads, crucifixes, guns, metal pots, knives, and bells like these.

HOW AN ARCHAEOLOGIST STUDIES THE PAST

Although an archaeologist can gain some information from artifacts that have been removed from a site, much more information can be gleaned through careful survey and excavation. During a survey, the archaeologist examines artifacts remaining on the ground and records large concentrations as sites. The archaeologist evaluates each site's size and age, and determines how it contributes to an overall understanding of Louisiana's past.

No two sites exactly duplicate each other, but some are more unusual than others. Some provide new or important information linking a group of people with a certain location or activity for the first time. This means that sometimes a small site, without elaborate or especially beautiful artifacts, may be more important to the understanding of the past than another site that is larger. An archaeologist who records an important site will recommend protection or excavation for it.

The archaeologist will evaluate threats to the site to determine the possibility of preserving the site intact. Some sites must be protected to insure that future generations can see unexcavated sites, and so that future archaeologists with improved techniques will have sites left to study. Even if an archaeologist excavates a site, he or she will usually leave parts of it untouched.

Archaeological excavation of a site is meticulous in order to preserve every piece of information. The archaeologist photographs and draws soil changes and artifacts as they are uncovered. This provides a permanent record of the relationships of materials to each other and to other parts of the site. Samples of charcoal, soil, bones, and decayed plants are collected for laboratory analysis.

Long months of study and interpretation follow excavations as the archaeologist and technicians piece together the many bits of information. Laboratory analysis may indicate what people ate, what plants were growing around the site, and perhaps even the date the site was used. Study of the artifacts may tell how the site was used, who used it, and whether they were trading with other groups.

Relationships of the remains show what parts of the site were used for butchering game, cooking food, making tools, gardening, building houses, burying the dead, and conducting ceremonial activities. Artifact 4 relationships may tell whether men and women worked in different areas, and whether the site was used repeatedly through the years. An archaeologist may even be able to discover very detailed information like whether the people cooked their fish whole or in fillets, what strains of corn they grew, and what kind of wood they used to build their houses. This detailed understanding can result only from careful study of a well-preserved site.

The archaeological sites of Louisiana span the time from the arrival of the earliest inhabitants, approximately 12,000 years ago, to the 20th century. These sites are as important in understanding Louisiana's past as original journals from early explorers. Each is a unique description of the land and people from years past. Just as a journal with all its pages tells more than a single page out of context, a complete site tells many times more than artifacts on a shelf or a site half-destroyed by modern-day construction activities.

Excavation of a mound site in Iberville Parish was meticulous in order to record the relationships of materials and to collect remains for laboratory analysis (above). Archaeologists were able to determine that under the mound was a circular house built of cypress and ash poles that were covered with thatch (right). Inside were interior support posts and wooden furniture such as beds or racks, as well as a central fire hearth and four smaller fire pits. Honey locust seeds, persimmon seeds and bones from four kinds of fish indicate some of the things these prehistoric people ate. Radiocarbon dates show that the structure was being used at A. D. 1000.

Everyone in Louisiana has the right to know about the state's legacy. The complete history of Louisiana can be recorded only through careful, detailed excavation by individuals especially trained in archaeological techniques. If a site is destroyed before it can be evaluated, that information is lost forever; it is irreplaceable. Unfortunately, sites are destroyed every day in Louisiana, both accidentally and intentionally.

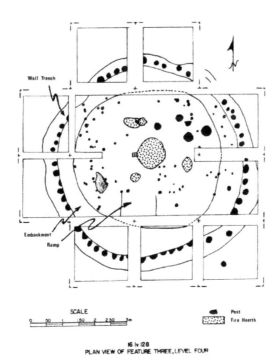

16 lv 128
PLAN VIEW OF FEATURE THREE, LEVEL FOUR

Wall Trench

Embankment

Ramp

Post

Fire Hearth

MAJOR IMPACTS ON SITE PRESERVATION

Throughout history, the traces of people who lived before have been altered by those who followed. Even when Indians camped in places where their ancestors had camped, they destroyed a piece of the record of their past. In contrast with this age-old pattern of minor alterations, however, is the potentially devastating impact of modern-day technology. In Louisiana today, major types of land modification include energy exploration and development, timber cutting, agriculture, urban expansion, waterway modification, and transportation network construction. These are all likely to disturb archaeological sites if they are conducted without care.

Heavy machinery can destroy a site in minutes.

The country's need for oil, gas, coal, and timber has accelerated the search for these products in the past decade. As exploration crews cut roads into otherwise inaccessible areas, previously undetected sites are exposed and disturbed. When heavy machinery is brought in to begin logging, drilling, or mining, sites can be gouged or crushed in a few seconds. Unless the crews are alert, fragile archaeological sites are destroyed before they are even recorded. In Louisiana's coastal areas, oil and gas production has also affected sites. Pipelines are often laid through piles of shells because they are more stable than the surrounding land. Unfortunately, a great many of these piles are man-made; they are actually archaeological sites.

Mechanized agriculture affects sites when plows turn up artifacts, jumbling the materials. Whenever an area is cultivated for the first time, sites may be found. In Louisiana, previously undisturbed areas within the river valleys are now being cleared for large-scale agriculture. Many buried prehistoric sites along old river channels could be destroyed. Sites in cultivated fields may be damaged further if they are plowed more deeply than in the past. Modern subsoilers can cut three feet into the ground, disturbing even deeply buried materials.

This gas pipeline in southeastern Louisiana's marsh was laid directly through an archaeological site.

Farmers often regard Indian mounds as troublesome when they occur in areas otherwise ideal for plowing. If farmers do not recognize the value of these mounds, they may have them removed. For example, a man in Madison Parish sold the dirt from a large Indian mound on his land for road fill. The ancient monument was removed so the land could be planted with soybeans.

Dirt from this mound in Madison Parish was used for a road foundation ...

Population growth in Louisiana has led to rapidly expanding cities and extended transportation networks. Modern cities are often in the same places that Indians and early Europeans built their settlements, so city growth is almost certain to disturb archaeological sites. As early as the turn of the century, archaeologists were charting the destruction of a mound group in eastern Louisiana. A city was growing up around one of the largest groups of mounds in the Southeastern United States. In 1931, an archaeologist wrote about the leveling of one of the mounds, a square multi-stage one, 80 feet tall and 180 feet on each side. The dirt was used to build the approach ramps for a bridge. Today, part of only one mound remains, protected because of the recent cemetery on top.

leaving behind only a few clumps of trees.

The destruction mentioned above has resulted from a lack of understanding of the importance of these sites. It has taken Louisianians a long time to realize the uniqueness and richness of their state's cultural heritage. While many people are now joining in the efforts to conserve the remaining sites, a few continue to willfully destroy them.

Some individuals dig into sites in order to find artifacts that can be sold to antiquity dealers. These looters have demolished entire Indian villages, stealing the story of those sites from all Louisianians. Even if the artifacts are eventually turned over to an archaeologist, most of the information has been obliterated. Lost are the records of where the artifacts originally came from, the relationships of the artifacts to each other, the samples of materials for laboratory analysis, and usually the ordinary or broken artifacts that tell the archaeologist much, but sell for little.

Looters at this archaeological site found artifacts, but destroyed all the other information archaeologists could have used to interpret the site.

GOVERNMENT HELPS

Although countless sites have been destroyed in Louisiana, many other sites have been saved by concerned individuals, companies, and organizations.

Our legislators have been interested enough in Louisiana's heritage to draft laws that help protect sites. Without a permit, it is now illegal to dig into, alter, or take anything from a site on state or federal land. Recent legislation calls for strict fines or jail sentences for people collecting materials from federal lands.

Our laws also help protect sites from those land alteration projects that in the past destroyed so many sites. The locations of proposed projects are now checked against archaeological records to be sure that no known sites will be affected. If the project is a large one, or if the area appears likely to have sites, an archaeological investigation will be recommended to determine whether sites are in the area.

Because of this process, approximately 400 previously undocumented sites are now recorded and evaluated by archaeologists in Louisiana each year. This has resulted in a more complete record of Louisiana's archaeological sites and a decrease in the rate of site destruction by industry. It has also encouraged developers to think about the care of our past early in the planning stages of their projects.

Both federal and state governments protect archaeological sites as parks that the public can visit. In Louisiana, the National Park Service has included the Big Oak Island site near New Orleans as part of Jean Lafitte National Historical Park. This site dates from the time of Christ and was seasonally used for shellfish collecting and processing. The Louisiana Office of State Parks also maintains two prehistoric archaeological sites that are open to the public and that have interpretive museums. One is Poverty Point Commemorative Area where the state's largest prehistoric earthworks were built 3,000 years ago, and the other is Marksville State Commemorative Area where Indians built mounds approximately 2,000 years ago. Archaeological investigations have also been conducted at many of the commemorative areas associated with 18th, 19th, and 20th century history. These parks give people a chance to learn more about archaeology and how it contributes to an understanding of our state's past.

BUSINESS AND INDUSTRY HELP

Businesses and industries are most likely to deal with archaeological sites when they plan projects on publicly-owned lands or when projects require permits. Many developers are sensitive to the need for preservation of important sites and plan ahead for evaluation of the project's impact on these. Businesses and industries whose projects will affect sites are proving to be creative in their responses. Sometimes, a minor change, like moving a road 25 feet to one side, may prevent a site from being destroyed.

Businesses also participate in archaeology because of curiosity about sites on their land. Some have provided food and lodging for excavators or have given grants to archaeologists to fund field and lab work. After analysis is completed, these companies have either donated artifacts to a museum or have developed small displays for their employees.

Companies are discovering that becoming involved with archaeology can have tax advantages. If a company donates land with a site on it to a nonprofit or governmental organization, the donation can be claimed as a tax deduction. A company also can receive a tax benefit by sponsoring excavation of a site either on or off its property. One southern Louisiana company funded 25% of the cost of an excavation and counted that as a tax deduction. The company owned the land with the site, so by donating the artifacts, it also could claim their worth as a tax deduction.

A New Orleans development corporation planned a massive project with an extremely important site in mind. The company leased land with a site on it to the Jean Lafitte National Historical Park for $1.00 a year. Rather than viewing the site as a liability, however, the company saw it as an asset. Through the lease of the site, the corporation generated positive community feelings, protected a part of our cultural heritage, and enhanced the value of the surrounding property. The benefits to the community and to the corporation will continue into the future.

A Baton Rouge company also was able to use archaeology in public relations. It developed an outstanding display about prehistoric Louisiana for the lobby of its main building. The exhibit attracts visitors and promotes interest not only in archaeology, but also in the company's services.

One New Orleans developer is protecting a major site and is advertising its decision.

IN BUILDING
NEW ORLEANS EAST,
SOME THINGS ARE MORE SACRED
THAN THE ALMIGHTY DOLLAR.

Once, New Orleans was rich in hidden archeological treasures. Over 600 prehistoric sites were buried throughout the city, but almost all of them have been destroyed in the name of progress. One of the most valuable sites, however, has miraculously survived the city's development: a prehistoric village of the Tchefuncte Indian Tribe, dating back to 500 BC. It's called Big Oak Island and it's located in New Orleans East.

In order to preserve this part of our city's heritage, New Orleans East has leased this 12-acre site, right in the heart of our community, to the Jean Lafitte National Historical Park. The cost: one dollar a year.

Donating this valuable piece of land to the Park Service is just one example of what makes us different from other developers. Throughout New Orleans East, we're leaving additional areas untouched as well, so that in the future, residents here will have trees to enjoy, birds to watch, and parks to play in. We're doing all this because we want New Orleans East to be a community that everyone in New Orleans can be proud of.

Building a community with this kind of concern for the environment may not be the most profitable development plan, but, like the treasures of Oak Island, it may very well be priceless in the years to come.

PRIVATE LANDOWNERS HELP

People who have archaeological sites on their land have many ways of protecting the sites. A site covered by natural vegetation usually is camouflaged and has limited access. As long as the owner does not clear the land, disturbance to the site will be minimized. A site already in a cultivated field probably will not suffer significantly from continued plowing at the same depth. Although initial plowing altered artifact relationships in the plow zone, the materials beneath remain well protected.

A landowner who is interested in protecting a site may want to have it recognized by placing it on the Registry of State Cultural Resource Landmarks. The Registry is established as an authoritative guide to the state's most important archaeological sites. Once a site is placed on the Registry, there is an agreement between the owner and the State of Louisiana to help protect it. This process ensures that important sites will be recognized, preserved, and protected to the maximum extent possible.

The site in this soybean field has already been disturbed, but probably will not suffer significantly if plowing is continued at the same depth.

Landowners who finance excavations can receive substantial tax benefits.

A landowner who is unable to protect a site because of plans to plow deeper, cultivate an unplowed area, or do construction, should alert the Division of Archaeology. If he gives enough advance warning, an archaeologist may be able to evaluate the site before the changes begin.

Recently, the tax advantages available to site owners have been clarified. One landowner paid half of the excavation cost at a site on his land and claimed his cost as a tax deduction. Later, he donated the artifacts from the site and also deducted their worth, equivalent to the entire cost of the excavation.

Federal tax incentives also apply to the gift of an important archaeological site to a governmental or nonprofit organization. This donation can be either an outright gift or an easement (in which the owner gives up certain control of the land, but retains ownership). In either case, the transaction qualifies as a charitable contribution for federal income tax, estate tax, and gift tax purposes.

YOU CAN HELP

Most archaeological sites are first discovered not by professional archaeologists, but by ordinary people who live or work near the sites. Usually these people do not know how to report a site to the proper authorities. If you find a site, you can help protect Louisiana's heritage by letting archaeologists know about it. The Division of Archaeology has prepared a form especially for you to use, and one is in the center of this booklet.

The first step in recording a site is plotting its location on a U.S.G.S. topographic quad or other accurate map.

You should fill out the form as completely as possible, without attempting to dig in the site. Mark its location on a map, and photograph the site area. Try to draw the artifacts you see; you don't need to be an artist, just trace around them on a piece of paper and sketch in any designs. If you find artifacts in a protected area where they are not being disturbed, it is best not to collect them; they may tell an archaeologist a great deal if they are left in place. If, however, you do collect something from the site, be sure to store it carefully with information about exactly where you found it.

Please mail the form, map, photographs, and drawings to the Division of Archaeology. Your information will be carefully reviewed, and added to the permanent file stored in Baton Rouge. A staff archaeologist will write a letter, telling you if the site has been assigned an official state number, and possibly asking for more information. By reporting a site, you will be helping to record the history of the state.

If you want to learn more about Louisiana archaeology, you can enroll in a class at a local university, visit museums, read archaeology books, or tour one of the state archaeological commemorative areas.

You may also want to join the Louisiana Archaeological Society (LAS). The Society's chapters throughout the state have monthly meetings with programs discussing local and state-wide archaeology. The LAS publishes a quarterly newsletter with information about current research, and an annual bulletin with in-depth reports. Often the LAS chapters also are involved in archaeological survey or excavation. The organization's members are both professional and avocational archaeologists who come together to advance Louisiana archaeology.

You will also find other opportunities to help protect Louisiana's heritage throughout the year. You can encourage your elected officials to support legislation protecting sites. You can help friends record and preserve sites on their land. Most importantly, you can explain to others the importance of archaeological sites, and the reasons for preserving them. By doing these things, you will be working with concerned people throughout the state to preserve Louisiana's legacy for the future.

Milton Keynes UK
Ingram Content Group UK Ltd.
UKHW050243220624
444555UK00005BA/507